By Jake Hunter and Aysha Imtiaz

The Next Generation Science Standards (NGSS) are reproduced with permission from the Department of Education.

By Aysha Imtiaz, Jake Hunter, Beth Hunter and Grant Cowell.

Seed Dispersion and Pollination: Seeds Are Special

Student Edition

ISBN 978-1-952346-47-7

 **Grade 2**
Next Generation Science

2-LS2-2 Ecosystems, Interactions, Energy, and Dynamics:
Develop a simple model that mimics the function of an animal in dispersing seeds or pollinating plants.

Lesson Anchor

Make a plantable seed-paper card

When was the last time you did something really nice for a family member? Now is your chance to do something kind. Write a letter to that person and decorate it for them with a seed-paper decoration!

What you'll need:

- a piece of paper (for your card)
- art paper or a paper towel (to make a flower)
- school glue, scissors, colored pencils
- Tobey tweezers
- seeds

Make a seed-paper flower:

Step 1: Draw a flower on your art paper or paper towel.

Step 2: Cut out the flower.

Step 3: Glue seeds to it.

Make a seed-paper greeting card:

Step 1: Fold and write a letter to a special person.

Step 2: Decorate it with your seed-paper flower.

Step 3: Deliver or mail the letter.

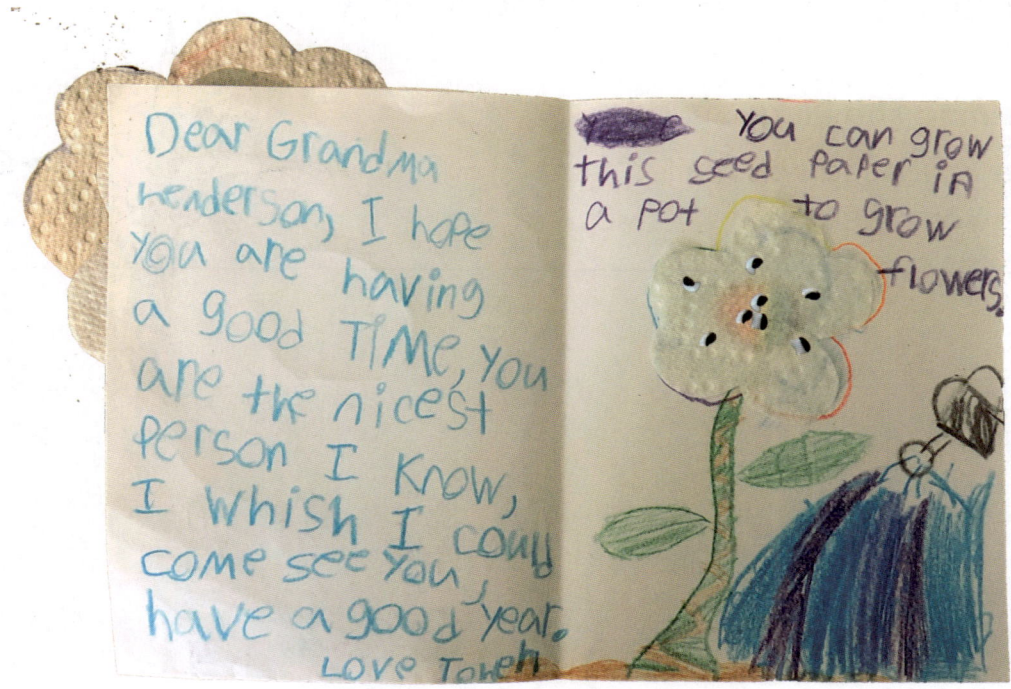

Dear Grandma henderson, I hope you are having a good TIME, you are the nicest person I know, I whish I could come see you, have a good year. Love Toueh

You can grow this seed paper in a pot to grow flowers.

When your family member gets your special card, they can remove the seed-paper flower you made and plant it outside. The flowers that grow will remind them of you!

Can you explain it?

 Think, Pair, Share!

How do animals in nature help transport seeds for plants?

Your seed greeting card's journey

By moving the seeds to a new place, you are doing the plant a favor! Because plants don't have legs and can't move on their own, plants need help to take their seeds to new places to grow up strong and healthy.

Draw a map showing:

- Where your seed was mailed from
- Where your seed went

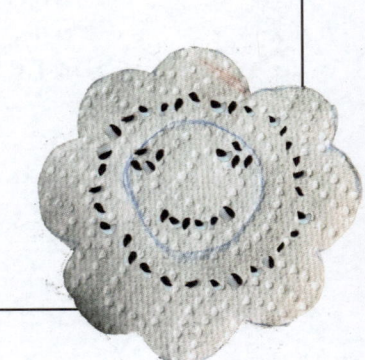

How did you help the plant by transporting its seeds?

_____

_____

_____

_____

How did the plant help you?

_____

_____

_____

_____

_____

How do humans or animals in nature help transport seeds for plants?

_____

_____

_____

_____

How many people could you fit in a city?

If the entire population of the Earth stood shoulder to shoulder, all 7 billion people could fit into a 500 square mile area. That's a little bit bigger than Los Angeles, California. Now, imagine what life would be like clustered together like that. Would you have room to play, eat or even lay down to go to sleep? No! There would be too many people all around you! People could not survive clustered together like that. We need space to move and live.

Describe how much space you would need to play a team sport.

_____

_____

Describe how much space you would need to grow a garden.

_____

_____

Describe how much space you would need to get some rest.

_____

_____

Think, Pair, Share!

Why would it be difficult for people to live clustered tightly together?

How many trees can you fit in a forest?

Plants or trees can't cluster too close together either. There wouldn't be enough space for all of them to grow up healthy and strong! Plants or trees would compete for soil, water— even sunlight! Plants need space for their roots to spread out under the ground to soak up water. They also need space for their leaves to soak in the sunlight. Spreading out helps to increase a plant's chance for survival.

Why would it be difficult for plants to live clustered tightly together?

_____

_____

_____

 Think, Pair, Share!

How far apart do plants grow in these places?

Plants in a garden

Trees in a forest

Bushes in a desert

Trees in an orchard.

The trees in this forest are spaced far enough apart that each can get enough light and water to survive.

Seeds and humans move to spread out

Seeds have an important task to accomplish. Their task is to get to a place where they have enough space to grow up to be a plant. Seeds need to disperse. Dispersal means to spread out and scatter. When humans need to disperse, they have many ways to spread out. Seeds, however, don't have legs. They have other ways to disperse.

 Think, Pair, Share! **In what different ways do humans move around?**

Draw different ways in which humans can move around.

What ways have you used to move around?

_____

_____

_____

Seeds can't move by themselves

Plants can't move around to spread out their seeds—instead, plants create seeds that are designed in special ways to be dispersed in nature.

Acorn

Cut out the seeds when you need them in the unit.

Burdock Bur

Dandelion Parachute

Blackberry

Think, Pair, Share!

What moves these seeds around?

Coconut

Maple Seed Helicopter

Mango

Touch-me-not seed pod

The shapes of seeds help them disperse

Every seed is different for a reason. Some seeds are hard and some are soft. Some are big and some are small. Some seeds have special structures attached to them that catch wind. Others are covered with tiny hooks that cling to an animal's fur. Some can float on water and other seed pods can even explode! Every seed has a unique design that helps it travel away from the plant that made it so it will have room to grow.

How do you think a milkweed seed is dispersed? Why?

_____

_____

A maple seed spins and drifts as it falls

Maple seeds are also dispersed by wind but they are too heavy to float in the air; instead, they flutter in the breeze. Maple seeds act like helicopters because they spin around as they fall. The spinning motion helps them fall slowly as they blow away from the tree that they came from.

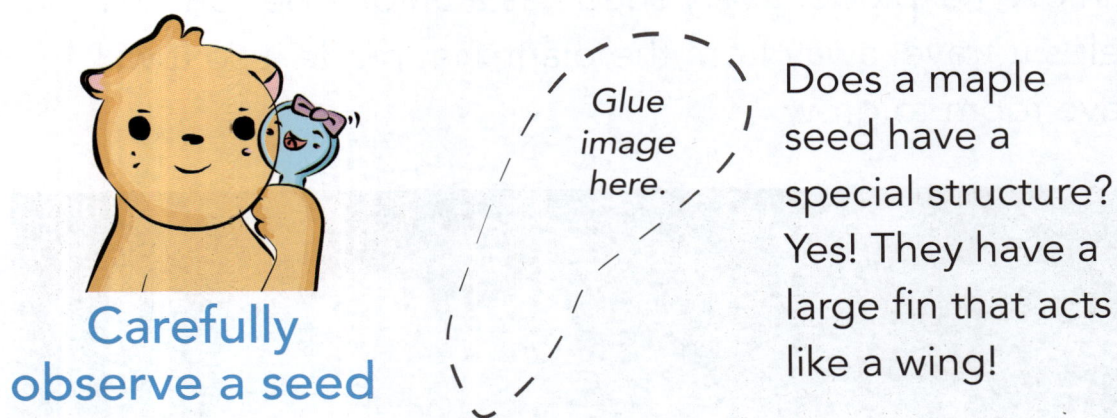

Carefully observe a seed

Glue image here.

Does a maple seed have a special structure? Yes! They have a large fin that acts like a wing!

Observe and measure the maple seed. Describe and draw the shape and structural features of the seed.

Size	Draw the Shape	Structural Features
Think of a word to describe the size of the seed.		

How are maple seeds well suited to be dispersed by wind?

_____

_____

Maple seeds blow in the wind as they slowly fall to the ground. The maple seed's fin also causes it to blow across the ground in the wind.

Think, Pair, Share!

What moves these seeds around?

Mimic a maple seed with a paper fish flier

Mimic how a maple seed is dispersed in the wind by making a paper fish flier. Just try to drop it straight down and you will see that it does quite a bit of fluttering before it touches the ground.

How far did it travel? _____

How is the flight of your paper fish flier similar to that of a maple seed helicopter?

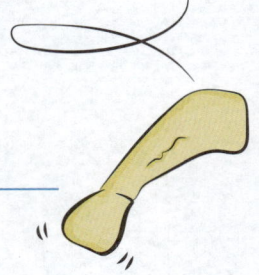

_____

_____

Did your paper flier travel far enough to disperse a seed? Why do you think so?

_____

_____

What you'll need:

- Scissors

What you'll do:

1. Cut out a strip of paper.

2. Cut on the dotted lines.

3. Attach the two ends together by joining the slots to make the shape of a fish.

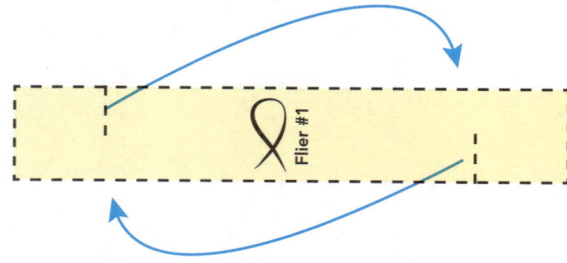

4. Drop the paper fish and watch it flutter.

Flier #1

Flier #2

Cut

Cut

Flier #2

Flier #1

Can you explain it?

Answer the question to show what you learned.

How do animals and the forces of nature help transport seeds to new locations for plants? Draw and explain.

Acorns are collected by squirrels

Round, heavy acorns fall straight down to the ground from an oak tree. So, how are acorns dispersed? By squirrels of course! A plump acorn is a tasty treat to a squirrel, so they collect them in their cheek pouches and hide them for later. When a hidden acorn is forgotten, it sprouts and grows!

Carefully observe a seed

Does an acorn have a special seed structure? Yes! Acorns are enlarged plump seeds! They attract animals!

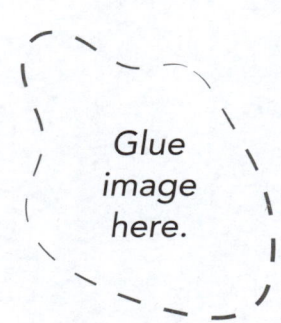

Glue image here.

Describe the size of an acorn. Describe and draw the shape and structural features of these amazing seeds.

Size	Draw the Shape	Structural Features
Think of a word to describe the size of the seed.		

How are acorns designed to be dispersed by squirrels?

_____

_____

Think, Pair, Share!

What moves these seeds around? How?

Squirrels often forget about acorns they save for later and the acorns sprout and grow.

Acorns are dispersed by squirrels who use the acorns as food. Squirrels gather acorns in large cheek pouches and hide the acorns to eat later in the winter.

A bur sticks to an animal's fur

Some seeds, called burs, are covered in tiny hooks that cling to the fur of animals. Burs easily fall off the plant when an animal brushes up against them and are carried away by the animal. By the time they fall off again, they can be many miles away. The seeds have a new environment to grow in.

Carefully observe a seed

Glue image here.

Does a bur have a special seed structure? Yes! Burs are covered with tiny hooks that stick to fuzzy things!

Describe the size of a burdock bur. Describe and draw the shape and structural features of these amazing seeds.

Size	Shape	Structural Features
Think of a word to describe the size of the seed.		

How are burdock burs well suited to be dispersed by animals?

_____

_____

22

Burdock burs contain seeds. These burs cling to the fur of animals or even the shoes and socks of humans. While tangled in the animal's fur, the seed can travel as far as the animal can walk.

Think, Pair, Share!

What moves these seeds around?

23

The Great Bur Experiment

Would you like to test how burs can travel and disperse by sticking to animals? Let's experiment with seed dispersion by making a model of how this process works. You'll tape paper burs to yourself and keep track of where they fall off you.

What you'll need:

- Scissors

- Tape

- Bur cutouts

What you'll do:

1. Cut out your burs.

2. Tape the bur cut-outs to clothing, jackets, backpacks and classmates.

3. Collect burs that fall to the ground and record where they were collected.

4. Wait for burs to be returned to your classroom by students from your school campus.

5. Estimate how far each bur traveled before it fell off and came to rest.

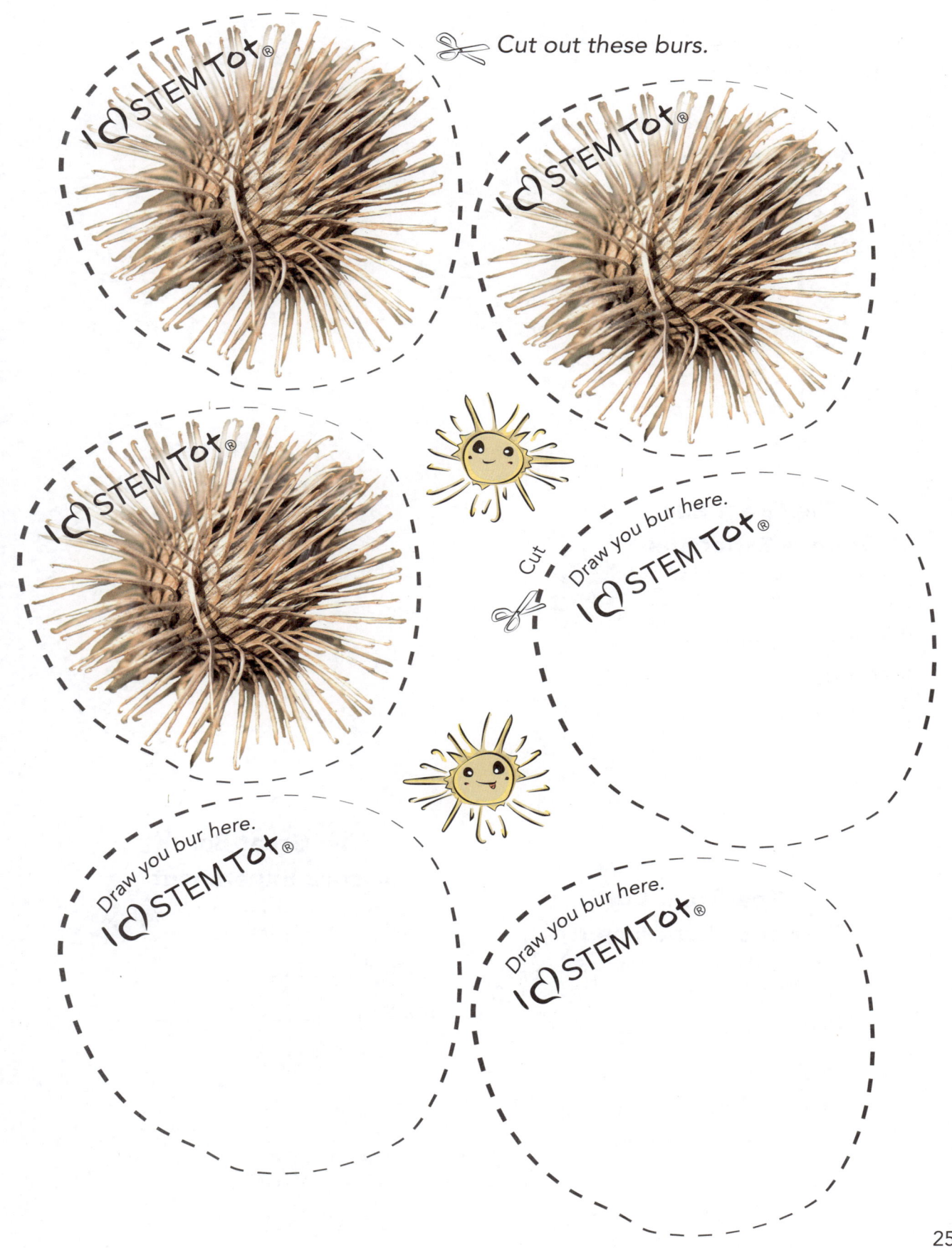

Cut out these burs.

I♡STEMTot®

I♡STEMTot®

I♡STEMTot®

Cut

Draw you bur here.
I♡STEMTot®

Draw you bur here.
I♡STEMTot®

Draw you bur here.
I♡STEMTot®

Fill out your name and your teacher's name on every bur.

The Great Bur Science Experiment

Return this bur to the front office or to this teacher:

Name:_____

Teacher:_____

Describe where you found this bur:

_____

_____

The Great Bur Science Experiment

Return this bur to the front office or to this teacher:

Name:_____

Teacher:_____

Describe where you found this bur:

_____

_____

The Great Bur Science Experiment

Return this bur to the front office or to this teacher:

Cut

Name:_____

Teacher:_____

Describe where you found this bur:

_____

_____

The Great Bur Science Experiment

Return this bur to the front office or to this teacher:

Name:_____

Teacher:_____

Describe where you found this bur:

_____

_____

The Great Bur Science Experiment

Return this bur to the front office or to this teacher:

Name:_____

Teacher:_____

Describe where you found this bur:

_____

_____

The Great Bur Science Experiment

Return this bur to the front office or to this teacher:

Name:_____

Teacher:_____

Describe where you found this bur:

_____

_____

Draw a map showing how far each of your burs traveled

Describe how far your paper burs traveled.

_____

How does 'The Great Bur Experiment' mimic the way burs are dispersed in nature?

_____

_____

How did you mimic an animal in your activity?

_____

_____

How did you mimic a plant in your activity?

_____

_____

Blackberries are eaten by animals

Sweet, plump blackberries are a tasty treat for small birds and other animals! Blackberries have tiny seeds inside them that birds and other animals don't even notice. The seeds have a tough outer shell that prevents them from being digested. With a full tummy, the bird flies away, and the seeds are excreted in a different location—this means the seeds come back out when the animal goes to the bathroom.

Carefully observe a seed

Do blackberry seeds have special seed structures? Yes! Tiny blackberry seeds are surrounded by a sweet, juicy fruit that attracts animals.

Glue image here.

Describe the size of a blackberry. Describe and draw the shape and structural features of these amazing seeds.

Size	Shape	Structural Features
Think of a word to describe the size.		

Why are blackberries well suited to be dispersed by birds?

_____

_____

28

Think, Pair, Share!

What moves these seeds around?

Delicious blackberries are food that attracts animals. Seeds inside the blackberries are then dispersed by the animals.

How far can an elephant carry a seed?

A scientist named Katherine Bunney was fascinated by how seeds are dispersed by animals. She fed elephants melons and collected their droppings so she could count the seeds and see when the last seeds were excreted. Katherine found that elephants can carry seeds up to 65 kilometers (40 miles)!

Elephants disperse seeds for fig trees in the Savannah. After eating fruit, the elephants walk long distances and drop the seeds far from where they came from.

This elephant is eating leaves, fruit and seeds. The elephants carry the seeds many miles before the seeds finally end up on the ground.

How far can a bird carry a seed?

Because of Dr. Bunney's amazing research, elephants are the winners for the furthest seed dispersing land animal. However, the award for the animal that can take a seed farthest goes to the migratory bird!

Birds such as this dusky flycatcher are known to disperse seeds over 300 miles, or 480 kilometers, through their digestive tract.

Credit: Kim White

A bird that eats berries can fly up to 300 miles (482 kilometers) before excreting the seeds.

How many seeds are in the bird poo?

_____

This bird poop contains seeds.

Delicious mangoes are moved by animals

Mangoes are a sweet, delicious fruit that animals love to carry around and eat. The mango seed, however, is very large and cannot be eaten. After an animal eats the juicy mango fruit, it discards the tough, inedible seed. The abandoned seed is likely to sprout with enough room to become a large mango tree!

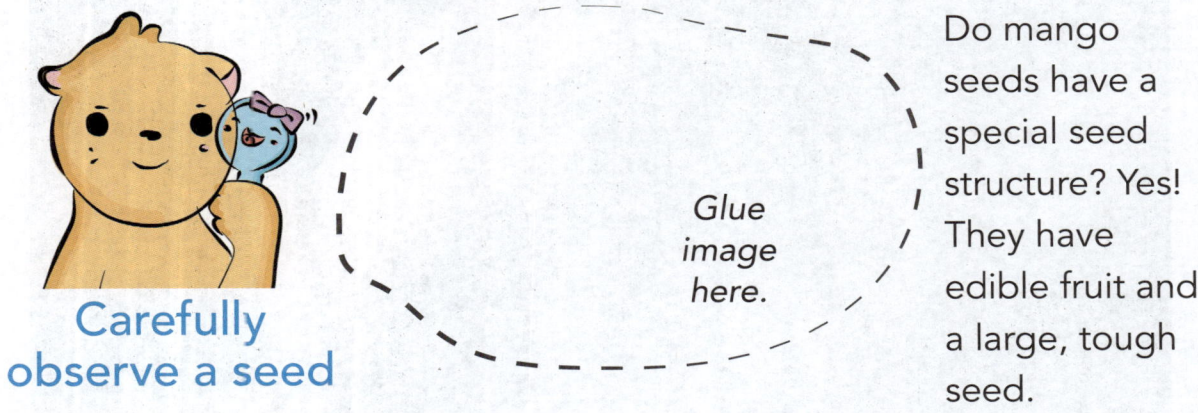

Glue image here.

Carefully observe a seed

Do mango seeds have a special seed structure? Yes! They have edible fruit and a large, tough seed.

Describe and draw the shape and structural features of the amazing mango seed.

Size	Shape	Structural Features
Think of a word to describe the size.		

How are mangoes designed to be dispersed by animals?

_____

_____

Mangoes attract animals because they are delicious. Their seeds, however, are not delicious. After eating the mango, animals throw the seeds aside.

Think, Pair, Share!

What moves these seeds around?

This monkey is eating a mango. How far do you think it could take the seed before it finishes eating?

A dandelion seed floats in the air

Dandelion seeds are so light, they can blow away in the breeze to land in fields or pastures far away from the plant they came from. These tiny seeds are ready to catch the slightest gust of wind with a little parachute that is attached to them.

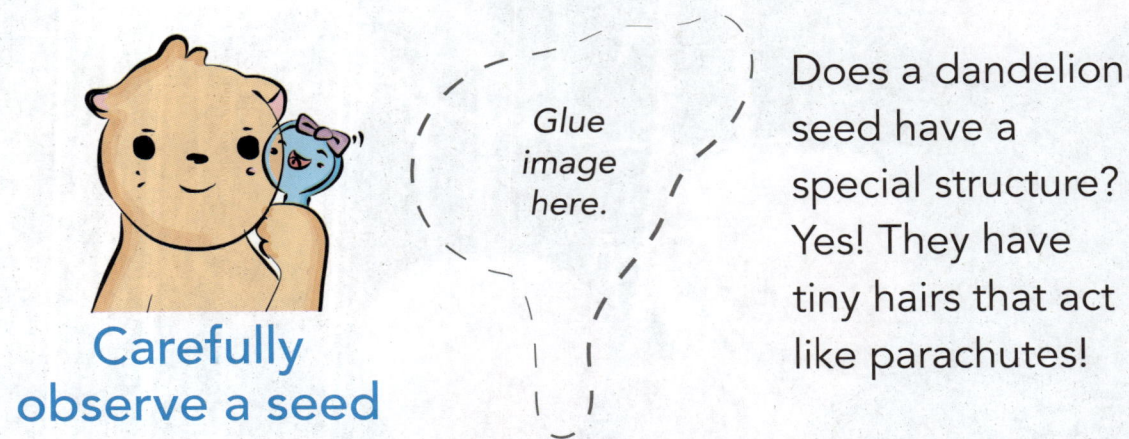

Glue image here.

Carefully observe a seed

Does a dandelion seed have a special structure? Yes! They have tiny hairs that act like parachutes!

Observe and measure the dandelion seed. Describe and draw the shape and structural features of the seed.

Size	Shape	Structural Features
Measure the seed here in this box. _____mm.		

How are dandelion seeds designed to be dispersed by wind?

_____

_____

What about these seeds allows
the wind to blow them?

Think,
Pair,
Share!

The seeds of a dandelion have little
parachutes that catch the wind.
These seeds can float away in the air.

The Origami Wind Catcher Experiment

Would you like to test how different shapes can catch wind and cause objects to disperse? Let's experiment with seed dispersion by making a model of how seeds are dispersed by wind.

What you'll need:

- Scissors

- Paper

What you'll do:

1. Cut out your origami wind catcher sheets of paper.

2. Fold an origami creation of your own to catch the wind.

3. Leave your creation on the ground outside.

4. Come back later and measure how far your origami wind catcher traveled.

The Scoopy Wind Catcher

The Origami Dragon fly

The Origami Maple Seed

The Origami Wind Catcher Experiment

Your Name: _____

What do you call your creation?

_____

Origami wind catcher #2

Your Name: _____

What do you call your creation?

_____

Today is your lucky day! You found an origami wind catcher that I am using for my science experiment. Please fill out the information below and return the wind catcher to the teacher listed here:

Teacher: _____

Describe where you found this wind catcher:

_____

_____

_____

_____

Please fill out the information below and return this wind catcher to the teacher listed here:

Teacher: _____

Describe where you found this wind catcher:

_____

Draw and label your wind catcher designs.

How far did wind catcher #1 travel?

_____

How far did wind catcher #2 travel?

_____

How does your wind catcher mimic a dandelion seed?

_____

_____

_____

How did you mimic a seed in your activity?

_____

_____

Coconuts float on water

A ripe, brown coconut is a seed that is hollow and floats on salty seawater like a boat. Coconuts are filled with a little air and a little water. The air inside helps the seed float. The fresh water inside allows the seed to sprout in places where fresh water is not always available.

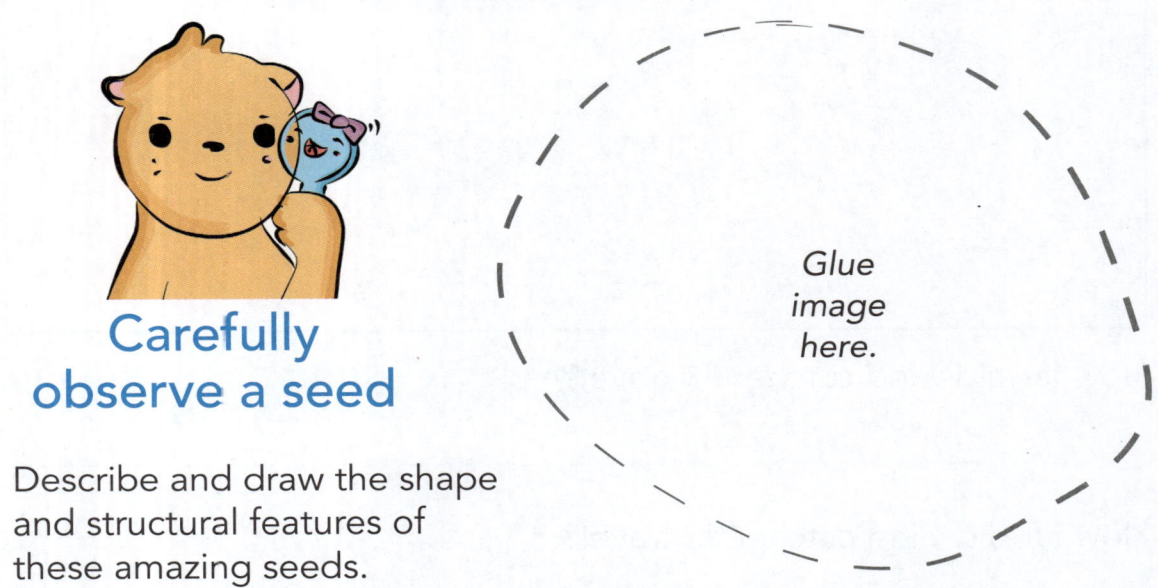

Carefully observe a seed

Describe and draw the shape and structural features of these amazing seeds.

Glue image here.

Size	Shape	Structural Features
Describe the size of a coconut.		

How are coconuts designed to be dispersed by ocean currents?

_____

_____

How do coconuts move from place to place?

Coconuts commonly grow on trees near the ocean. Since coconuts can float, they can travel from one island to another on their own.

Touch-me-nots pop to spread their seeds

Some seed pods, such as touch-me-nots, can explode. The fibers in the pod naturally want to curl up, but the seed pod is long and straight. As the pod dries, it builds tension and becomes ready to POP! Eventually, the seed pod pops, kind of like a mini-explosion which scatters the seeds as they fly high into the air.

Carefully observe a seed

Glue image here.

Do touch-me-nots have seed structures to help them disperse? Yes! They have an exploding seed pod.

Describe and draw the shape and structural features of these amazing seeds.

Size	Shape	Structural Features
Measure the seed in the picture. _____ mm.		

How do touch-me-nots disperse their seeds?

_____

_____

42

Popped Seed Pods

Seed Pod

Seeds

This touch-me-not has already popped. Only a few seeds are left in the pod. The rest of the seeds were scattered around.

Think, Pair, Share!

What moves these seeds around? How?

IT'S SONG TIME!

Phew! There are a lot of ways that a seed can move around! To remember them all, we are going to play a dancing game. Get ready, seeds, because today you will move and groove to this seed song! Sing to the tune of "**Rain, Rain, Go Away**".

What you'll do:

Learn the verses and plan a dance move for each verse.

Step 1: Sit quietly. Wait to hear which song cue your teacher will call.

Step 2: Jump up and sing the verse while you do a seed dance to show how your seed moves.

Step 3: After you finish your song and dance, plop down to get planted. Stay seated quietly on the floor until your teacher calls out the next cue.

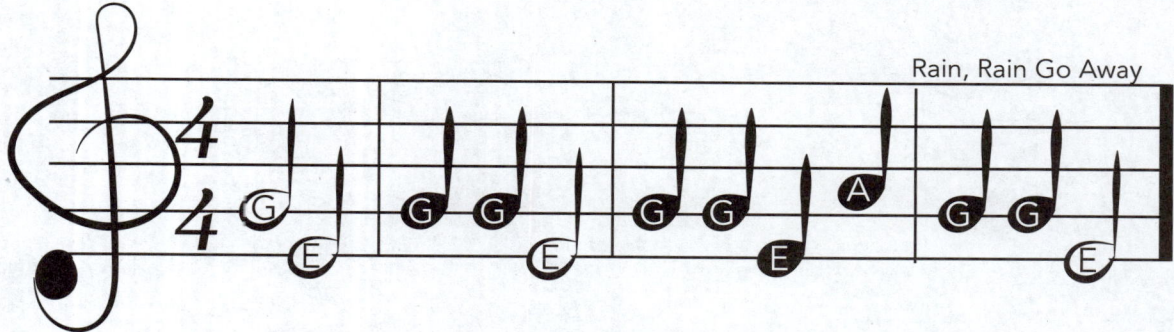

Seed, Seed, Blow Away!

When you hear your cue, jump up and sing the verse and
do your song actions to show how your seed moves.

Song Cue: Blow Me Away!

Seed, seed, blow away

With their wings they dance and play

In the wind seeds want to play

Seed, seed, blow away

Dance move: Flutter
and twirl around.

Song Cue: Blow Me Away!

Dance move: Wave your
arms like ocean waves.

Seed, seed, float away

Like a boat they're on their way

In the waves they drift and sway

Seed, seed, float away

Song Cue: Tag-along Hitchhikers!

Seed, seed, stowaway

In fuzzy fur they stick and stay

On animals they ride away

Seed, seed, stowaway

Dance move: Crawl on
all fours like a puppy!

Song Cue: Yum, Yum! Gulp it Down.

Dance move: Rub your
tummy and run in a circle!

Seeds, seeds, in fruit they stay

Eat some seeds and walk away

In your tummy they're okay!

Seeds, seeds, in fruit they stay

This student is observing her seeds under the microscope.

Go on a seed hunt to discover seeds

It's time to walk outside to search for seeds! You can find seeds just about anywhere. See what seeds you can find and observe them to tell how they are dispersed.

What you'll need:

- a Tedros test tube or a small collection bag
- school glue
- a microscope (or magnifying glass)

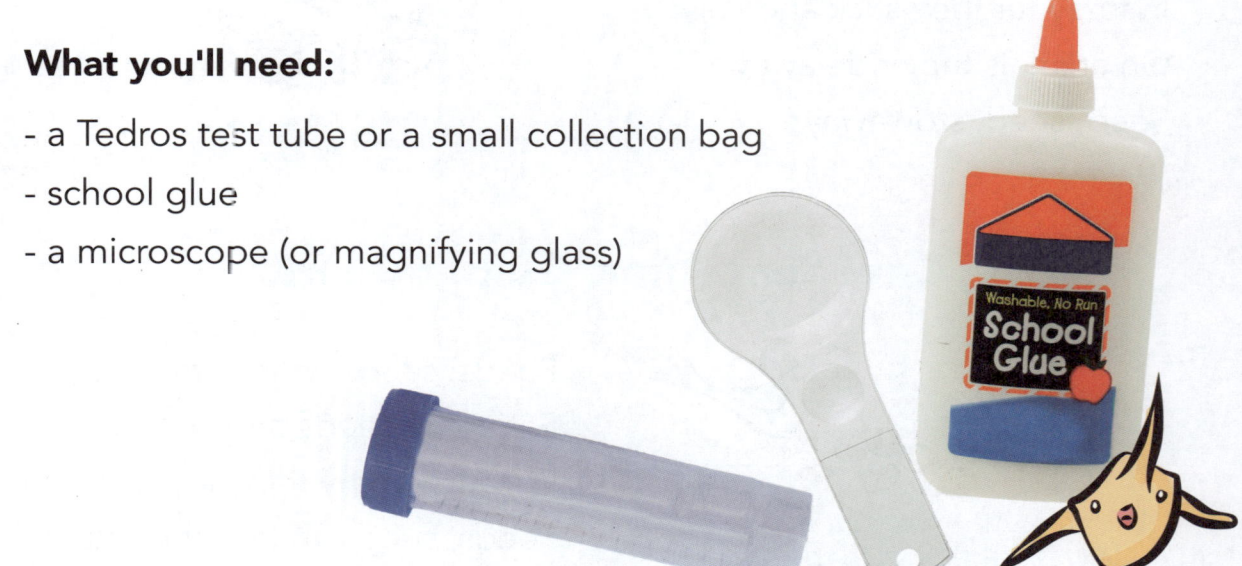

What you'll do:

Step 1: Go outside to collect and discover seeds.

Step 2: Bring the seeds back to your classroom to observe and describe their special structures.

These students collect seeds.

This student observes and sorts her seeds into dispersion categories.

3. Sort the seeds into categories according to how you think they are dispersed.

4. Glue your seeds to your worksheet.

This student glues seeds to his worksheet.

My Amazing Seeds
See my seed walk discoveries

Explore your school grounds and look for seeds. Sort your seeds according to how they disperse and glue them to your worksheet.

These seeds can fly
(Glue seeds here)

These seeds can float
(Glue seeds here)

These seeds stick to animals
(Glue seeds here)

These seeds are eaten by animals
(Glue seeds here)

Draw the special structures that you found on your seeds.

Explain the
Phenomenon

Can you explain it?

Explain how your seeds are dispersed.
Why do you think so?

_____

_____

_____

_____

What interesting structures do you see on your seeds?

_____

_____

_____

Seeds Are Special!

Soupy SUPER SEED

Once upon a time, Soupy Super Seed wasn't quite as super as he is today.

Hey mom, I'm pretty super, aren't I?

No baby ... We're pinto beans.

We can't run, we can't fly, we can't stick to anything. And we taste really bad too!

Sadly, it was true ...

Bobby! eat your beans!!!

No. YUCK!!

Soupy didn't exactly taste like powdered donuts.

But Soupy didn't just sit around feeling sorry for himself! Soupy set out to ...

Watch out!

... become a master of water.

... a master of stealth.

Huh?

... a master of wind.

Yee-haw!

And he got armor to protect himself and powdered sugar to make himself taste good too.

Mmm... Tasty.

Now Soupy wasn't just an ordinary pinto bean anymore!

All seed powers combined!

FLOATY

Now Soupy was **really** super.

Are not!
Am too!
Are not!
Am too!
Na ah!
Uh huh!
Not super
Oh yes, I am super now!

And so, he changed his name from "Soupy" to "Super."

Hi Soupy

Mmmm...

Oh sorry, what was it again? Scoopy. Right?

Mmmm...

Super Seed would dedicate the rest of his life to going on adventures ...

Where's that rabbit when you need it?

... um, kind of. Where did that rabbit go? Super Seed needs a ride. Remember? He still doesn't have any legs.

How does Soupy travel by water?

_____

_____

_____

_____

How does Soupy travel by wind?

_____

_____

_____

_____

What two ways can Soupy travel by animal?

_____

_____

_____

_____

Think of another super-power for Soupy that mimics a seed. What is it?

_____

Draw and label the super-power here.

How does the new super-power work?

_____

_____

_____

_____

What seed does the new super-power mimic? How?

_____

_____

Make your own Super-Seed comic. Write and illustrate!

How does Super-Seed attract an animal to himself?

How does Super-Seed finally hitch a ride out of town?

Show Super-Seed riding inside or outside the animal.

Super-Seed finally reaches his new destination.

Where does Super-Seed end up? How far did he travel?

Super-Seed had finally reached his destination. Did he make it to the right place? Does he like where he ended up? Is this pinto bean really cut out to be a super hero? We are about to find out!

How does the story end? How does Soupy use his new super-power?

Animals and insects pollinate plants

Plants also depend on animals to pollinate their flowers. Plants can't shake, bend or move to pollinate themselves. Instead, plants have to attract insects or animals to visit them in order for their flowers to be pollinated.

This butterfly pollinates a flower as it sips sweet nectar.

Pollen Anthers *are covered with pollen grains the size of dust.*

The Stigma: *When pollen grains touch the stigma, the plant is pollinated.*

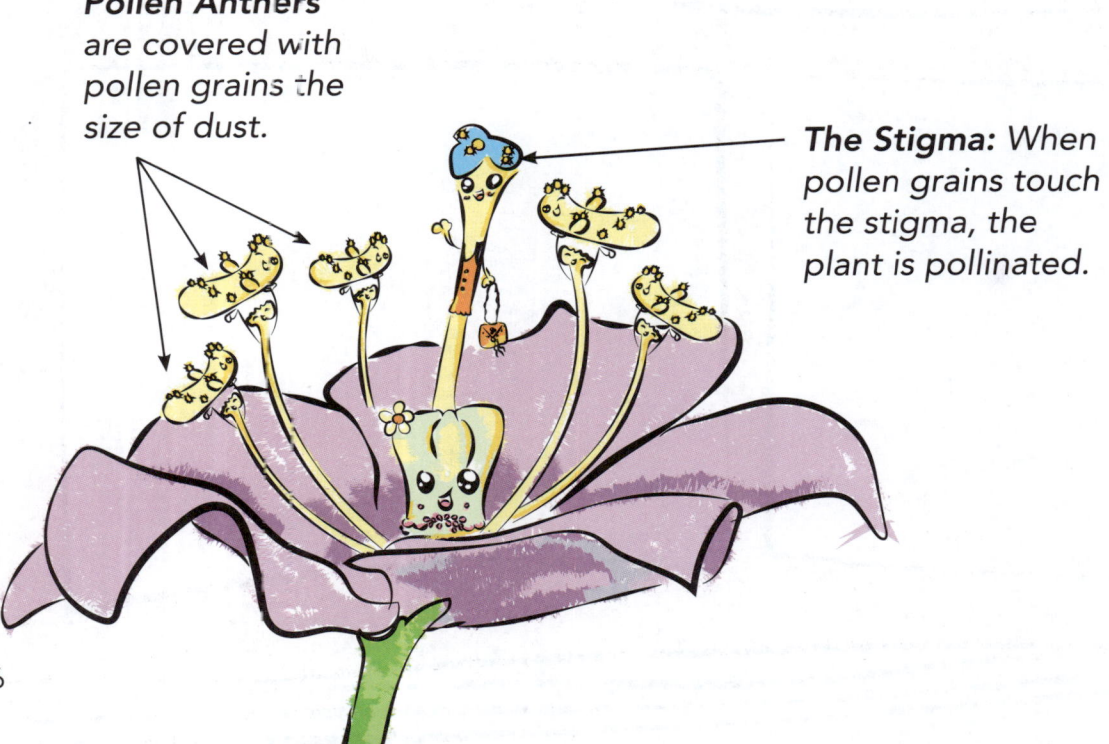

Think, Pair, Share!

How can this flower be pollinated?

Here, you can see the parts of a flower involved in pollination.

Bees have fuzzy hairs all over them

To attract animals and insects, flowers give animals food such as pollen or sweet, yummy nectar. As insects and animals search for this food, they pollinate the flowers. Bees have fuzzy legs and bodies that pollen can get stuck to as they sip nectar. When they move to the next flower, they take pollen along with them all over their bodies.

This bee has hairs that are covered in tiny yellow pollen grains.

What special structures and abilities does a bee have that makes it a good pollinator to plants?

_____

_____

_____

Hummingbirds have long slender beaks

Hummingbirds have wings that allow them to hover and long, narrow beaks, which allow them to drink nectar. When they drink nectar, pollen gets on their beak. As a hummingbird goes from one flower to the next, they pollinate each flower.

This hummingbird has a long, slender beak that pollen grains stick to.

What special structures and abilities does a hummingbird have that makes it a good pollinator to plants?

_____

_____

_____

Fun-Dixie Journal Entry

What was your favorite part of this learning unit?
Draw and write about your experiences.

**Royal
STEMTaught Post**

When you read a great chapter in the STEMTaught Journal and do
the fun activities inside, sometimes you just want to write about it!